Women of War

Women of War

Jeff Dawson

Women of War

1055 Regal Row #314 Dallas, TX. 75247.

ISBN: 978-1-7321547-2-8, print

Introduction

I came up with the idea for this work while watching, "We Were Soldiers Once." The scene where Harold Moore's wife was going door-to-door delivering dreaded Wester Union Telegrams. It dawned on me that there are very few books devoted to the women who served, worked or waited home for their men. To me, it is one of the most powerful cinematic moments in a war film.

Our women, have served, worked, died and cried untold tears to help defend and preserve the freedoms of our great country. They truly are the backbone of our great nation.

I hope I have done them justice with this tribute.

Mr. Dawson is the author of over eighteen works. His memoir, dedicated to his high school sweetheart, "Love's True Second Chance" was awarded the seal of approval from the IndiePendent Association for exemplary story writing. A full list can be found at the end of this work.

He currently live in the Dallas/Fort Worth Area.

Women of War

Women of War

Jeff Dawson

Women of War

Table of Contents

Women of War

Christmas Homecoming?

Wondering if this will be the year.
Will we spend it together as a family,
or will I again perform both duties?

It's been over a month since I heard a word.
The message wasn't reassuring.
His unit was in heavy combat.
The newspapers said the war
was on the verge of being won.

Neighbors were making preparations for
the upcoming victory.
People were upbeat, displaying smiles
they'd hidden for years.

I maintained my reserve.
This wouldn't' be the
first time the papers were wrong.
I secretly hoped they were right,
History told me; trust my own gut.

Amongst the gay feelings,
Jenny called to tell me

Women of War

her Tom wouldn't be coming home.
He was MIA.

I told her how sorry I was and would help
anyway I could.
Inside, I was thankful it was Tom
and not Roy.

Am I wrong for feeling this way?
Am I being selfish I want Roy by my side?

The phone rings. It's Joyce.
Willy is KIA.
I fight back the tears and keep up the brave
face I've become accustomed to wearing.

My thoughts are interrupted by our children.
"Mommy. Was that Daddy on the phone?
Is he coming home this year?
We miss him so much."

"Children, I don't know.
Go make sure all the lights
Are working. Daddy would like that."

"Yes, Mommy."

Women of War

I light up another cigarette
and pour another cup of coffee.
I'll never get used to the waiting.
I've only learned how
to deal with hope
so the children don't worry.

What will I do if he doesn't return?
How will I act
if he comes home broken?
How will I support our family?
Will I remarry?

Will the children call him Daddy?
Where will we live?
How many times have I thought of those
options?
I've lost count.

My parents said they would take us in.
His folks said they'd do
whatever they could.
They mean well, but I know better.

Many of my friends tell similar stories.

Women of War

In the beginning, the host family is
sympathetic and understanding.
They try to understand our loss and despair.

Yet, as time moves forward they realize they
have taken on a burden
they are ill equipped to deal with.
The loss and pain are foreign to them.

The children's fitful, sleepless nights
become haunting.
The void of a family learning to cope
can't be trivialized with ice cream,
gifts or movies.
The random outbursts and
times of silence scares them.
In the end,
they fend for themselves.

Will that be me?
I pray it won't,
What guarantees,
do I have? None.

"Mommy. We're finished.
Come see what we did."

Women of War

I take one more drag, one more sip of coffee
and join the children.

"Daddy will be so happy
when he sees what you've done."
They smile with acceptance.
I hope it's so.

There's a knock at the door. My heart jumps
into my throat.

Is it him?
Is it a neighbor bearing bad news?
Is it the army chaplain?
Is it Western Union?
Or is it, Roy?

Fear keeps me frozen.

"Mommy. Someone's at the door? Are you
going to answer it?"

I try to move my feet; they don't respond.

My heart aches to know
what or who is on the other side.

Women of War

Is it Roy? Could he really be home?
I have to know but the fear keeps me from
moving.

"Jenny, you and Tommy go see who it is."

They run to the door, flick the light switch
on and slowly open it.

I almost faint with the shadowy figure filling
the frame.
My senses go numb.
My mind stops working.
The sight frightens me.
I recognize him but I'm not sure.

"Mommy, it's Daddy. It's Daddy!" the kids
scream.

Is it really?
My eyes focus as he enters the foyer.
He looks thinner, more serious,
a little more muscle,

But yes it's him.
He flashes his familiar smile and winks.

Women of War

It is him! It's Roy!

I rush to hold him in my arms.
I hide my tears of joy.
For I know one terrible truth
the children don't know,
this could be our last
Christmas together.

War stops for no one.

DADDY

I remember the first time
I uttered those words.
I think I was two or was it three: dada.
He pulled me close and kissed me.
"I love you too."

The next I was six and it really hurt.
I fell off my bike, scraping my knee.
"Daddy, it hurts so bad."
He picked me up and kissed me.
"Honey, it'll be okay."

The next time was more dramatic,
Well of course, I was fourteen.
"Daddy, we were only holding hands."
"I know honey,"
"Son, don't break her heart."

"Daddy," I cried. "He doesn't love me
anymore."
"It's okay, honey. I still love you."

Women of War

He said I could do it. I wasn't sure.
I wanted to make him proud.
I couldn't wait to walk across the stage,
And wave my diploma yelling,
"DADDY, I DID IT!"
I know I heard him yell out,
"YES YOU DID, HONEY!"

Today, I say it for the last time.
"Goodbye, Daddy."

Distant Eyes

It was a life none could comprehend.
Like a trooper,
he returned to hallowed ground, kissing it,
grateful for
surviving,
but saddened for those who didn't.
He went to college, obtained a job,
married his love then
started a family.
Yet, no matter how calm or normal
he appeared on the outside,
his eyes held a distant look.
He moved through the corporate ranks,
working hard to provide for his family.
He performed all the obligatory
functions a good father and husband would
do.
No matter how busy his life,
I sensed a silent pain.
I remember the day he spoke of the past.
We were sitting on the patio.
He stared off as he sipped his tea; me, my
wine.

Women of War

"Dad?" no reply. "Dad?"
A tear slid down his cheek.
"Jimmy, the medics are coming. Hold on.
Hold on Jimmy. Don't die on me."
His creased lines were covered with tears.
The eyes were no longer empty. They were
alive with the past in the present.
It was the only time he spoke of it before
passing on.
If not for his actions, tortured dreams,
memories and distant eyes,
I question whether I would be free
to write his epitaph.

Found then Lost

Despite my orders,
she left.

The battle was hours old.
The outcome still in doubt.
But the wounded had to be treated.

The first reports were grim.
"Fifty percent casualties and mounting.
Position being held.
Medics down."

I knew she was listening.
Damn woman never liked
Following orders,
much less accepting them.

I made it clear, they must hold.
We couldn't spare another soul.
They must do what they must
to survive.

No one knew how long she'd been gone,

Women of War

Only that she was gone and I knew where.

I gathered a small detail and headed out.

I'd lost count over the past months we
worked together how many boys
she'd saved or soothed
as their final curtain fell.

No matter how dire the patient's
prognosis was,
her magnetism kept them focused on her,
rather than their wounds.

Thirty minutes later,
we were met with a challenge.
The correct call name was provided.
The private led us to his lieutenant.

Taking care to keep noise
and silhouettes low.

We entered the cramped,
muddy command post.
"Lieutenant, where is she?"

Women of War

His eyes panned across the darkened, blood-
soaked field
"She was there."

I tried many times to dissuade her from
going out.
She would admonish me by asking, 'How
many would you like to die?'
"None," was my answer.

He took a deep breath,
removed his helmet rubbing
his frayed hair.

"I gave her two men to assist. She crawled
out, tended to the wounded
then motioned when they were stable.
Two men would go out to
retrieve the soldier.

I lost count how many she found and
patched-up."

Tears starting tracking
down his grimed face.

Women of War

"Where is she?"

"The last man had a head wound.
While the men were dragging him back,
she positioned herself between the sporadic
fire and the wounded.

They were less than three feet
from the trench.
I was helping them into
the ditch
when a single shot sounded."

Instead of finishing his thought,
he pointed to his left.

I could barely make out the row of soldiers
toiling over others.

I moved over to them,
checking on their status.
When asked how they were,
instead of replying
they looked to the right.

My eyes followed theirs.

Women of War

"Sir, if it weren't for her
None us would be alive.

The unmistakable strands of blonde hair
Had tumbled out from her
cracked helmet.

He Promised

I can't stand it,
The not knowing,
The anxiety of waiting!

I spend my days shopping,
Cleaning, cooking and waiting.
The radio adds no solace,
Only more angst!

Two years, he's been gone.
Pride swelled my breast as
He and thousands like him,
Headed off to fight the Nazis.

He promised he'd return.
He promised he'd take care of me.
He promised he'd write.

Three weeks and not a word.
Is he dead, wounded or MIA?
The waiting is killing me!

Should I keep burning a candle?

Women of War

Should I remain vigilant?
Should I tell the children?
Tel them what?

Your father is never coming home.
He'll never teach you how to play catch
Or ride a pony or see you graduate or
Walk you down the aisle.
The waiting is killing me!

Last Patient

I looked about the sparse
operating room;
took in the stench of death,
blood-soaked earth.

Piles of dirty bandages,
empty IV bottles,
spent syringes,
a multitude of
flesh-covered implements
used to patch their battered bodies.

A kaleidoscope of colors:
black, white, yellow, brown, red;
the dominant one—red.

Images of faces flickered,
flashing through my mind.

I tried to remember all
who filled the beds:
Kenny, William, Joseph, Jamal,
Harry, Lou, Yu and others.

Women of War

The room began spinning,
my feet, legs, no longer responding.

Lights dimmed.
Senses dulled.
A wave of warmth
covered me,

My lifeless body became
no more.

I am – the last patient.

Last Plane Out

I made the trip
more times than I could count.

I wanted to travel,
see the world.
Never realizing the trauma.

Seven thousand miles back and forth.

We were the buffer for
the nightmares they hid.

Pain welled up in my soul as they
recounted their tales of fallen
brethren.

Cries of battle filled the
Metal capsule.
For some it was an escape from hell,
for many, a casket in disguise.

My colleagues would whisper
Trying to understand, why they did it.

Women of War

It seemed senseless; the waste of
America's youth.

I wanted to console them,
tell them it would be okay,
But their young, hollow eyes,
worn, haggard faces,
told a story we'd never understand,
until the final flight.

We were pulling out.
The boys gave everything,
yet it seemed in vain.

The jungle and country
were littered with their
friends— and comrades;
broken dreams and bodies.

They'd given all for God and Country.
But for what? Freedom?
Democracy? Victory?

We sat on the tarmac waiting. Waiting for
what?

Women of War

I looked out the small window—shocked!
Medics, nurses, doctors
scrambled around a bus.

One by one, reappearing.
Each carrying a small package.
What were they cradling,
with such compassion?
What could be so important?

They dropped their precious cargo in seats,
or removed a row,
replacing them with small open containers.

Tears filled my eyes, realizing why
they fought and
died—children.

My Dearest Betty

December 25th, 1944

I apologize for not writing, my love.
For the last few weeks,
I had nothing to write.
The snow is endless
The cold is like nothing I've ever felt,
or wish to again.
Many of my men are wounded
or frozen.
I hoped I'd be home for Christmas,
but the Germans had other plans.
I guess they think they can still win
this damnable war that has taken
you from my arms.
I wish I could express how much I miss
and love you each day, but paper is in
short supply and writing is a difficult chore.
I don't want you to worry
and I don't want you to feel sorry.
We are fighting a just cause,
I only wish it were over.
It sounds like Jerry's getting ready for

Women of War

a final push.
My darling, Betty. I love you and look
forward to the day we reunite.

Your loving husband,
Robert

January 6th
Mrs. Betty Richardson,
We're sorry to notify you that your…

Tears drench the telegram.

Nurse!

I always wanted to serve.
My mom told me it would
Be the hardest most rewarding
Job I'd ever perform.

She told me of Bastogne and Normandy.
She talked of the men she'd nursed back
To health.

Yet there was always something in her
Eyes, telling a tale she couldn't speak.

Thirty-Six Hours

Is it day or night?
I forget.

The bodies continue to roll in.
Broken legs, eviscerated bowels,
punctured lungs, cracked ribs,
ruptured spleens, severe head trauma,
vanished jawlines, crumpled shoulders
and blood.

It was a sea to itself. No matter how many
we saved and repaired, the carnage
Never stopped.

Like cordwood, they came rolling in.
Boys. They were only boys!
Hours, minutes, seconds ago,
they teemed with the energy of youth.
Now, their dwindling reserves are
summoned to survive.

"Nurse. Nurse. More plasma."
I retrieve the last bottle.

Women of War

Will it save this boy
Or will he be another casualty?

I bear not the thought.

Waiting 1965

I remember our last night together.
Many of my friends couldn't understand
why I didn't screw his brains out.

They all said they would have.

But what did they know?

Their boyfriends were stateside
on college exemptions or left behind
with medical leave.

Their men would always be close.
Mine was going overseas.

He was assigned to the 1st cavalry.
His commander addressed the unit,

"Men we are going into combat.
We are going to be in harm's way.
Many will not come back, but many will."

I appreciated his honesty.

Women of War

Jimmy knew he'd be one who returned.
Yet, neither of us could see the future,
So instead of making love,
we spent the night in each other's arms—
praying

I received a letter two months ago.

Jimmy was all smiles in the photo.
He told me how proud he was to serve with
such a fine unit.

They'd suffered some casualties,
but so far he'd been lucky.

Two of his comrades, Billy and Ray were
killed in the
Battle of Ia Drang.

He asked if I'd stop by
and see their folks.

I wrote back, I would,
when we could go together.

Two more months and five letters later,

Women of War

I hadn't heard from Jimmy.

The seconds on the clock ticked away.
Each day, longer than the last—waiting.

We Served

Under its breath,
our country called.

We asked not what the job
at hand would be,
only that our help
 was required.

We filled shops, factories and
The military.
We never questioned our ability, desire,
patriotism or mission.

Filled with excitement and anxiety,
But never worried about performing.
It was our time to shine.

To show the dominant species
we were more than mothers or housewives.
More than trophies to be dressed and taken
to parties.

We were a force to be reckoned with.

Women of War

Those of us who joined the WAC's
were the cream of the crop.
Our love for flying
left them no abandon.

Sneered and jeered by our male peers,
we never lost faith.
Knowing we were equal to men
in the air,
kept our spirits high.

No, we weren't allowed to fly over the
battlefields
of Europe and the Pacific,
but we cheered our comrades
in arms in Russia. They were proving
their worth against the Nazi aggressors.

Many paid the ultimate price
pulling air targets or ferrying
planes across the US,
to Britain and islands in the Pacific.

How did our country honor our dead?
By having us gather the
funds to help families pay for the burial.

Women of War

We had no benefits.
Our pay was half of the men's.
Did it infuriate us? Did it leave us
despondent and bitter?
At times.

But knowing we were on the front lines of
the war zones homeland
Filling the roles men couldn't or wouldn't,
was our reward.

We were the backbone
of the revitalization of the American
military.
We were the ones
who did the heavy lifting and riveting.

We were the ones
suffering in the factories and mills,
churning out the implements
and tools of war.

We were cutting, forging, casting,
the components of:
ships tanks, jeeps, planes and submarines.

Women of War

WE WERE THE AMERICAN
WORKFORCE!

On VE and VJ day, men and women
cheered and hollered.
The papers lauded our great
accomplishments in the titanic struggles
against dictatorships and imperialism.

They proudly claimed how "Our Boys are
Coming Home!"
We cheered with them,
but we knew one thing,
our country, right or wrong
would take decades to recognize.

Without us, OUR country
 could not have won the war.

Western Union

As a civilian, they were welcoming words'
Followed by good news.

In 1968, that changed for me.

As a wife, girlfriend or mother of a soldier,
They were the last words we wanted to hear.

They were the most feared
words in the English language.

Instead of bringing good news
from a relative or friend announcing
a wedding, promotion, birth or new
residence,
it harbored the dread of Mac, Bobby, Jim or
John,
not coming back.

The girls I spent time with, shared a
common thread.
Our men were serving in the Marines, Navy,
Air Force or Army.

Women of War

We banded together for support and
understanding.

None of my old acquaintances understood
my feelings.
They went to the malt shop, had their hair
done,
Attended weekend matinees, or cruised the
streets with their friends.
They didn't understand and never would.

They didn't know the distant stares,
of worry or concern, my friends and I
shared.
How could they?
They were caught up in their narrow
comfortable worlds of self-absorbing
frivolity.

They silently laughed behind our backs,
yet when face to face they exhibited
their unwarranted pleasantries.
They would never understand.

We stayed together, providing comfort
and support for ourselves.

Women of War

Our men didn't want the war.
They didn't have a choice.
Their country called and they answered;
they were *real* men.

They didn't question politics or the obscure
reasons sending them seven-thousand miles
away.
They went for each other. They would fight,
suffer and die for each other.

And we would wait.
Wait for a phone call,
a Chaplain or even worse, Western Union.

Yes, the call, "Western Union Man,"
froze the blood in our veins.

For many it was the sound of joy,
for us, it was death incarnate.

And so, we wait.

Which Side is Right?

Claire wept when she read the headline

"War!"

Euphoria swept the country!
War had been declared.
Young men couldn't wait
to answer the call
They dismissed the words of
old men who had served on the fields.
The stories they told couldn't be that bad.
If they were, why did they still have
their old, worn, musty uniforms and
tarnished medals?

It was a new day! A Bold day!
A day when boys would become men.
They would go to fight and win.
They would be hailed as heroes.
Their chests would be emblazoned with
shiny new medals showing the world
what brave deeds they had performed.

Women of War

She held back tears as the young men
flocked
to the recruiting stations.
She'd seen it before.
Her tears would be saved for those who
needed them

Three years passed.
The casualty lists grew longer.
The populace no longer cheered
with news from the front.

Small mounds of dirt stretched
beyond her sight.
She wiped blood from her hands onto an
apron that could handle no more.

Many times, doctors asked her to find a
fresh one.
She graciously refused.
It was her badge of honor and remembrance.
Her name was on everyone's lips.
Her compassion, caring and love
knew no bounds

Cries and moans broke her out of her trance.

Women of War

She looked back over her right shoulder.
The sight would sicken a normal person.
Rows of wounded, maimed and dying
filled her vision.

The days of excited and boisterous men
crying out for victory, no longer
sounded for them.
Uniforms held no color for it had long faded
away from the blistering sun
and blustery, winter winds.

To her, they were all the same.
Young men, who were so sure of themselves
littered the ground with broken
bodies and spirits.

They called out to their mothers,
wives and girlfriends
hoping that somehow they'd be reunited.
For them, it mattered not which side they
were on,
only if they would live and be whole again.
It no longer mattered, "Which side is Right."

For them, she shed her tears.

The Picture

How many times have I looked at it?
I've carried it around all these years,
The edges are frayed and worn,
The image is faded.
We were so young once,
and happy!

You were so stunning in your uniform
I wore my mother's wedding dress,
something borrowed, something blue.
We never thought our
time would stop.

As I write this, I remember the songs from
those carefree days:
"Seasons in the Sun,"
"Slow Dancing,"
"He Stopped Loving Her Today."

Tears cascade onto the paperwork. They are
joyful remembrances, not sorrow.

Women of War

You talked of coming back and being a
rodeo star!
"Amarillo by Morning" just finished
playing. It takes my breath away.

When I imagine you in a tight pair of
wranglers and your worn cowboy hat.
My God, you were so handsome !...and then
you were called up.

We put our lives on hold until you came
back. But you didn't. You couldn't.
My life was so empty until our son entered
the world.
I promised myself, he would know you, if
only in spirit.

I held many jobs and never regretted a one.
They kept us fed, clothed and sheltered
Times were hard, and some days, I didn't
think I could go on, but I had to.
For you, Jack Jr, and myself.
God, how I miss you!

When James came into my life,
I was scared to death.

Women of War

Over time he assured me
he would accept me, Jack Jr, and your
memory into his home.

With time, I slowly relaxed and let him
bring down the walls I thought were
sheltering me from more hurt.

I knew I was with the right man when he sat
me and Jack Jr down.
"Jack, would it be all right if I married your
mom? But, before you answer,
would you ask your dad too?"

I must have sobbed for an hour when Jack
beamed up and said,
"Daddy and I agree. You will make a great
father to me and the best husband Mom
could find."

Many times our children would catch me at
the kitchen table, smoking a cigarette,
drinking a cup of coffee, cradling *The
Picture* and crying.

Women of War

Seldom did they intrude. Rather, they look
to Jack and James for guidance and an
explanation. The reply was always the same,
"Mother is having a moment. Give her time
and she'll be back."

"What is she holding in her hands that
makes her so sad?"
"Someday, you'll have to ask her. But not
today."

I never let on I heard them talking about me.
I would pull myself together and place the
photo back in
my pocketbook and return to the present.

Twenty years passed. We were as happy as a
family could be. James and I supported them
in all their endeavors whether they be:
sports, arts or academics.

James planted a garden under my kitchen
window with different colored roses for each
family member. That lush purple one?
That's you.

Women of War

The day Jack Jr graduated from high school I was left breathless. When he walked across the stage I saw him standing by your side smiling and then you looked up and waved at me.

When we came home I cried for an hour. Jack Jr. and James walked into the kitchen and sat at the table. They both placed a hand on mine, holding *The Picture*.

Jack squeezed my hand. "Mom, I felt him too."

I sobbed uncontrollably. "James, I'm so sorry. After all these years, it shouldn't affect me like this. I'm so sorry."

He wiped a few tears from my face; brushed a few tear-soaked strands of hair away, then looked deep in my eyes. "Sweetheart, we all love you."

I tremble as the love of this man fills me with strength.

Women of War

He hasn't replaced you, but he has planted a
garden in my heart, once empty and barren.

The kids are all grown and have lives of
their own. James passed a few years back,
but then I think you knew that.

I see my life flash by, a lush garden that
grew from love.

I reach up, turn off the lamp, cradle your
picture and take my final breath.

I'm coming home.

Inspirational Daily Thoughts

Monday
Embrace what you have today rather than fear about what you wish you could have tomorrow.

Tuesday
Sometimes the answers to our questions are so clear, we can't see them.

Wednesday
Why is it when we seek clarity and receive it, we question its simplicity?

Thursday
When we dwell on what we don't have, we overlook everything we do have.

Friday
Why are there more reasons not to take action than reasons to act?

Women of War

Saturday
I will no longer enter debates of futility, for in the end, they are futile.

Sunday
It isn't necessary to continue driving in the ruts when the next lane is freshly paved.

Monday
Reaching the horizon isn't the goal, it's the quest.

Tuesday
A mountain conquered is only the beginning.

Wednesday
If one continually strives for perfection and excellence, they never see their accomplishments.

Thursday
True clarity is revealed when we eliminate our own smokescreens.

Women of War

Friday
When we focus on positive thinking,
negativity has no room to reside.

Saturday
Positive ideals result in positive actions.

Sunday
How can we love another when we've
forgotten how to love our self?

Monday
When one comes to understand their true
self, they will no longer think of what they
don't want.

Tuesday
When we focus on what *we* want, our
subconscious *will* negate what we do not
want.

Wednesday
If today was the first day of your life, would
you follow the path less traveled or the one
well worn?

Women of War

Thursday
It is not possible for us to help others when
we ourselves need to be helped first.

Friday
When our thoughts are filled with
negativity, it is not possible to appreciate the
positive.

Saturday
Why is it we want to help others when we
haven't helped ourselves first?

Sunday
When we clear our mind of irrelevant
clutter, we make room for the desires we
want.

Monday
All we desire is only a request away.

Tuesday
Today is the first day.

Women of War

Wednesday
Why is it when we search for answers to our questions, we ignore the response?

Thursday
A clear mind allows new beginnings.

Friday
Setting aside fifteen minutes a day allows us to clear our thoughts and focus.

Saturday
Each new day takes you closer to your ultimate goals.

Sunday
When we understand clarity, our goals become clear.

Monday
We will never achieve our desired goals if we allow the mistakes of the past to guide our way.

Women of War

Tuesday
In order for us to chart a new path it is
necessary to remove all negative influences.

Wednesday
If you wait for tomorrow to correct the
mistakes of today, the path you want to
follow will never materialize.

Thursday
If we associate ourselves with those who
have no vision, then we too, shall watch ours
fade away.

Friday
When focus is obtained, our goals become
much clearer.

Saturday
The goals for tomorrow begin today.

Sunday
Knee jerk reactions will result in knee-jerk
results.

Women of War

Monday
If we consume our lives focusing on matters
of trivia, it is not possible to achieve our
essential goals.

Tuesday
New beginnings require new patterns of
thinking.

Wednesday
Do not let a negative situation define who
you are.

Thursday
If you're going to use your past experiences
to achieve your goals, make sure you're
using the correct experiences.

Friday
New beginnings are only a positive thought
away.

Saturday
Poor choices don't define us, they allow us
to learn how to make wiser choices.

Women of War

Sunday
Mental health is as important as physical health. It only takes a few minutes in the morning to prepare us for the coming day.

Monday
Positive thinking is the first step to igniting a new beginning.

Tuesday
If you don't take the first step towards a new fulfilling life, nothing will change. The choice is yours.

Wednesday
Those we closely associate with, is our own reflection. What do you see in your mirror?

Thursday
When we forge our path based on other's opinions, it no longer becomes our path.

Women of War

Friday
When our minds are clear, we shall not fall
victim to those who attempt to pull the wool
over our eyes.

Saturday
Not every thought is required to instill
groundbreaking ideas; what is important is
that it's your thought.

Sunday
If we don't start working on ourselves first,
tomorrow will be a repeat of yesterday. The
power and choice is yours!

Monday
We are all masters at creating distractions in
order to avoid addressing difficult decisions.
Imagine the heights we'd achieve
channeling positive energy to positive
decisions.

Tuesday
Spreading fear, manifests fear. To be aware
is to be wise.

Women of War

Wednesday
How can we be discouraged with our present path, when we allowed others to map it out?

Thursday
If we allow adversity to overwhelm us, we will never see our path.

Friday
It is the individual's responsibility in determining their self-worth.

Saturday
If we wonder why we aren't attracting those we wish to congregate with then we aren't sending out the correct vibrations.

Sunday
If we continue to complain about past failures, our path will never change.

Monday
When we realize we are the ones stopping us from achieving our goals, it allows us to

focus, and correct the mindset that's been holding us back

Tuesday
Unwanted drama is the key to being deprived of your true self.

Wednesday
Small talk only leads to small ideas.

Thursday
When you feel others have you sinking in their quicksand, you can continue to listen and sink or reach out to the rope.

Friday
It is time to stop trifling over issues of inconsequence; focus on issues which will begin a new, prosperous journey.

Saturday
Adversity only makes us stronger if we learn from the experience.

Women of War

Sunday
Strife is only magnified if we continue to feed it.

Monday
Never be afraid to call on a higher power to help heal the pains of the past.

Tuesday
Freedom is more than a word, it's a way of life when there are men and women willing to sacrifice so much for so many.

Wednesday
How can circumstances improve when we aren't willing to improve ourselves?

Thursday
A new path is only successful if it's accompanied by a revitalized attitude.

Friday
Instead of wasting energy identifying the faults in others, we should divert the energy and work on our own shortcomings.

Saturday
Giving up on hope means, we have given up
on ourselves.

Sunday
Positive thoughts and attitudes WILL result
in positive actions.

Monday
Failure is never the final outcome; it's a
stepping stone to success.

Tuesday
New beginnings come with a price—
success!

Wednesday
The only reason others say it can't be done
or achieved is because they either don't
share your vision or are too afraid to strike
out on their own.

Thursday
Never take for granted the most wonderful
gift you enjoy each and every day—life.

Women of War

Friday
When we honestly give thanks to others,
they will reciprocate in kind.

Saturday
Not every inspirational thought is intended
to be a commentary on how we shall live
our lives; it is a map for moving us in the
right direction.

Sunday
Acceptance is gained when we accept
others.

Monday
Solitude is a time to reflect and work on
ourselves; friendship is a time to celebrate
what we've learned.

Tuesday
Happiness is not a product of those we
connect with, it's a product of our own
mindset.

Women of War

Wednesday
If you find yourself questioning your self-worth based on what others are saying, it's time to find those less judgmental.

Thursday
Complaining about your current circumstances will change nothing.

Friday
Knowledge and understanding are not gained by talking, they are achieved by listening.

Saturday
If you aren't willing to change your current state of mind and find the positive force in life, everything will remain the same.

Sunday
Positive thoughts will not pan out if we question their outcome.

Monday
Take a breath, smell the roses, enjoy life; it's the only one we have.

Women of War

Tuesday
Destiny, fulfillment, happiness are only
words if we only discuss their merits.

Wednesday
Temporary setbacks should not be viewed as
failing; they are the first steps towards
success.

Thursday
It's not important how others view us,
what's important is how we view ourselves.

Friday
We cannot succeed if we continue to
question our self-worth and our unique,
exciting characteristics! The choice is yours.

Saturday
Never let the doubts of others guide your
decisions.

Sunday
If we spend our hours and days attempting
to gain support from our friends and peers

Women of War

for the path we know we should take, we
have wasted valuable time pursuing our
dreams.

Monday
Each day is the beginning of a new path, if
you choose it.

Tuesday
It's never too late to begin your new
journey. Taking the first step can be the
hardest. Let today be that day.

Wednesday
Focusing on improving ourselves will then
allow us to help others.

Thursday
When we fill our heart and mind with joy
and peace, those we want to surround
ourselves with will more easily be drawn to
us.

Friday
Our goals will only be achieved if we
choose to work on them each and every day.

Women of War

Saturday
The definition of success is not what others perceive it to be; it's what *you* believe it to be.

Sunday
Burdening others with our problems in an effort to make ourselves the center of attention and sympathy does nothing to allow us to move forward and work on the real issues. Seeking out help is one thing; complaining about circumstances is another.

Monday
How many times have you asked, "When will I be inspired?" Inspiration comes when the mind is open to new thought processes.

Tuesday
Our dreams are only obtained when we discipline ourselves to take action and enact on the plan we prepared.

Wednesday
It's never too late to start fresh if you are willing to embrace a new and clear mindset.

Women of War

Thursday
No matter how difficult our current path is,
if we maintain a positive outlook and
attitude, *we* shall overcome the odds!
Friday
Positive actions *will* lead to positive results!

Saturday
Inner peace will only be achieved when we
are able to eliminate outside, negative forces
and concentrate on our goals.

Sunday
If yesterday didn't turn out the way you
planned, do not let it interfere with today's
new path.

Monday
Believing in your own self-worth is the first
critical step in beginning a new start.

Tuesday
No one will believe in you unless you do it
first.

Women of War

Wednesday
Our answers are only a question away.

Thursday
Those who talk the most know the least.
Friday
One must consider who they are talking to
so they understand the message.

Saturday
Debating an issue with closed minds only
results in a pyrrhic victory.

Sunday
How does a society progress when everyone
is right and no one is wrong?

Monday
The darkest days are the ones when no one
acknowledges the building storm.

Women of War

If you enjoyed the story, please do not hesitate to post a review on Amazon, Goodreads or any other site of preference.

List of books by Jeff Dawson
Gateway: Pioche, Science fiction
Destination D.C. Book Two of the Gateway series, Science fiction
Target Berlin Book three of the Gateway series
Occupation, WWII Alternative history
Sabotage Book two in the Occupation series
Terror at the Sterling, horror
Love's True Second Chance, Memoir
Why Did Everything Happen?, Memoir
The Baseball Coaching Manual: Little League to High School. Volumes I & II, Instructional
Goober and Bill, Humor
Final Delivery, Suspense short
Catfished: Jeff and Julia's Saga
Catfished Again: Jeff and Naughty Nadia's Saga
Guinea Pigs of the 70's and 80's
Living with Breast Cancer-Speech presentation

Other works available through LDDJ
Enterprises Publishing
Angelic Answers: Love Letter for Daily
Life, Kathryn Magee, Spiritual
Collection of Erotic Romantic Encounters:
by, Savanna Payne
Cracking Up! J.J. Reinhardt

You can follow me at:
Twitter: @Jeff Dawson59
Facebook:
https://www.facebook.com/jeff.dawson.184
or https://www.facebook.com/pages/Loves-
True-Second-Chance/201274679901838
Facebook:
https://www.facebook.com/pages/Occupatio
n/231877123504847?ref=hl
Facebook:
https://www.facebook.com/pages/Baseball-
Cadillac-Power-Hitters-
Association/125677220828234?ref=hl
Facebook:
https://www.facebook.com/pages/Why-did-
everything-
happen/146270185426560?ref=hl
Website: http://jeff-dawson.blogspot.com/

Women of War

Email: LDDJEnterprises@gmail.com or
Jdawson41@netzero.net
Amazon link: http://www.amazon.com/Jeff-Dawson/e/B0054DRYIO/ref=sr_tc_2_0?qid=1394463163&sr=1-2-ent

Upcoming releases:

Cauldron 3rd book in Occupation series

www.ingramcontent.com/pod-product-compliance
Lightning Source LLC
Chambersburg PA
CBHW071422040426
42445CB00012BA/1258

*9 7 8 1 7 3 2 1 5 4 7 2 8 *